Non Profit Doesn't Mean No Profit

Changing The Portrait Of The Humanitarian Grind

Asiya Nasir

Asiya Nasir
3848 N Gratz St
Philadelphia, PA 19140
862-258-5447
utopianenterprisebizsolutions@gmail.com
www.utopianenterprisebiz.com

"The Non-Profit Masterclass was amazing! I learned, and re learned so many things. I will be reaching out to you for more help in the future!"

- Dr. Demi Fauziyyah Abedo-Adelaja, Founder of The Aafiya Project headquartered in the DC metro area.

"I highly recommend Asiya Nasir of Utopian Enterprise Business Solutions! She is so thorough, and the quick turnaround is an understatement."

-Becky Leese, Founder of Unity Collaborative headquartered in Williamsport, PA

"The Non-Profit Masterclass was an AMAZING class. The best part is the way you have confidence in your students and encourage us. You are an amazing instructor. I will be looking to take more classes to stay motivated!"

-Zilfa Baksh, Founder of Raffaz House of Worship and Learning Center headquartered in Queens, NY

"The Non-Profit Masterclass helped my organization ABC Reads get it together!!! She helped us with getting our internal structure in place which was something we were really struggling with. She also assisted with amending our Bylaws for us to run the organization efficiently. I highly recommend her services.

-Sasha Beckette-Abdullah, Founder of ABC Reads headquartered in Cleveland, OH.

"I truly felt connected to the information you teach. You took time to explain the little things that really add up to big things. Your attention to details is appreciated."

-Nyshia Brooks, Founder of Black Butterfly Societe headquartered in Mansfield, OH.

"I highly recommend Asiya Nasir of Utopian Enterprise Business Solutions…she is so thorough and the quick turn around is an understatement."

-Becky Leese, Founder of Unity Collaborative headquartered in Williamsport, PA

"Thank you so very much for hosting such a dynamic webinar this evening. I truly felt connected to the information you were teaching. You took time to explain the little things that really add up to big things…which could cost a business money or opportunities. Your attention towards such details is appreciated."

- Nyshia Brooks, Founder of Black Butterfly Société headquartered in New Jersey

"Thank you, Utopian Enterprise Business Solutions and Asiya Nasir, for supporting my wife and I with completing our Non-Profit paperwork. This consultant is patient and helpful!"

-Bilal Ahmad, Co-Founder of Urban Seeds Grow headquartered in East Orange, NJ

"Thank you for all of your help and inspiration. I'm so very excited, we have nothing but great things ahead to share with the world. If anyone is looking for the best by far consultant company, reach out to Asiya. She is beautiful both inside and out, she is genuine and very professional and her knowledge is invaluable."

-Khadijha Muhammad, Founder of Blossom Next Level headquartered in Philadelphia, PA

Dedication

I dedicate this book to all the aspiring Founders and existing Founders of Non-Profit organizations. To those who strive to fill a void in their local communities or around the world. I dedicate this book to those who search tirelessly for funding sources so that your organization can be the answer to someone's cry for help. This book is dedicated to those who live intentionally in championing a cause, for a purpose greater than themselves. This book is dedicated to you for saying YES…

Acknowledgements

I would like to acknowledge my gratitude to Allah (swt) first and foremost for decreeing in my life the gift of transforming lives and inspiring others to see themselves in a higher light then when I met them. Thank you for answering my du'a/prayer to be used by you in any way you saw fit. THANK YOU

I want to acknowledge my family for always supporting my work and the long hours it takes away from them in order to do the work that I do, you are truly my biggest cheerleaders. I appreciate and love you so much for it. THANK YOU

I want to acknowledge my closest friends and you KNOW who you are for always being my sounding board on my days that I do not always feel balanced. Thank you for keeping me grounded.

I want to acknowledge my past coaches who "saw" me then and to my current coach who "sees" me now. To my current coach for stretching me in ways that I feel like I am in a yoga class each week. I thank you for placing a mirror before me and assisting in my growth for the moments you and I live for…the aha moments! THANK YOU!

Lastly, I want to acknowledge my clients and students who allow me to stretch them. I thank you for allowing me to be part of your story and your journey. THANK YOU!

About the Author

Asiya Nasir, Founder and Non-Profit Strategist of Utopian Enterprise Business Solutions, builds strong foundations for newly established nonprofit organizations and takes existing nonprofit enterprises to their next level.

The founding of her nonprofit **J**ourney to becoming and **E**xtraordinarily, **S**trong, **S**uccessful **I**ndividual with **C**ourageous, **A**spiration, known as J.E.S.S.I.C.A Cares, coupled with her background in business development, staff management and financial services, makes her uniquely qualified to assist nonprofit managers with setting, achieving, and exceeding their goals.

Her approach is vastly different than that of other consultants. She doesn't believe in one-size-fits-all plans. Instead of simply managing strategies and offering suggestions, Asiya helps her clients learn to enjoy the journey as it unfolds. This leads to greater understanding of the entire process and ultimately deeper success in a shorter period of time.

Asiya provides support through each step of the process. From the initial consultation meeting and goal development stage to strategic planning sessions and plan implementation phase, she is passionate about helping clients turn their dreams into reality.

About the Author continued

As a specialist in the business development field with more than 25 years of experience in the financial industry, Asiya's knowledge and guidance are invaluable. She coaches, mentors, and inspires clients to give 100 percent on the job every day. Her enthusiasm for her work and ability to inspire others lead to maximum performance for her clients. In addition to providing staff and volunteer resources, she also conducts fundraising and board development workshops.

She knows what it takes to operate a successful nonprofit organization and pushes her clients to expect the unexpected and become comfortable with the uncomfortable. As her client's biggest advocate, she does what it takes to help their vision take shape. Asiya is widely respected and well known for her nonprofit efforts. Asiya also became a certified Fundraising Specialist and Grant Writer in 2020.

She self-published her first book, *Mirror Mirror on The Wall… Who Am I After All* in December of 2018 and has been a featured author for various nonprofit newsletters such as Project Rousseau and Angel Wings Bridge Foundation. Asiya has also received many honors – most recently the Berkely College Women's Empowerment Award in 2021, the United Nations Woman of Impact Award in January of 2019. In addition, she was presented with the PATH Award from Ma'oon Inc. in 2018 and has earned numerous local community achievement awards, including County College of Morris, EOF Mentor Program (2016), Face My Abuse, Women Who Make A Difference (2015), Morristown Neighborhood House: Appreciation for Service and Dedication to the African American Community (2012), Berkeley College: Featured Success Student/Changing Lives for 80 years (2011) and Project ReDirect Family Services: Excellence in Business and Community Service Award (2011).

Contents

Chapter 1: The Proper Mindset When Starting a Non-Profit 1

Chapter 2: The Myths of the 501c3 Tax Exempt Status 9

Chapter 3: Creating and Building Upon a
Winning Board of Directors 19

Chapter 4: The Heart of Your Non-Profit: Volunteers................... 31

Chapter 5: Creating a Corporate Culture as
A Charitable Organization 41

Chapter 6: Does Anyone Know Your Story? 49

Chapter 7: Think Outside the Box: Secure the Funds 57

Chapter 8: Nurturing the Donor Relationship 63

Chapter 9: If It Don't Make Dollars, It Don't Make Sense:
Money Management 71

Chapter 10: The Burn Out: Work Smarter, Not Harder 77

CHAPTER 1

The Proper Mindset When Starting a Non-Profit

"If you set goals and go after them with all the determination you can muster, your gifts will take you places that will amaze you."

– Les Brown

Non-Profit organizations are amongst the most misunderstood businesses in existence today. Unfortunately, even many nonprofit founders also misunderstand the purposes of a nonprofit. Due to a lack of understanding, nonprofits are placed in a "second class" status when ranked amongst other business entities. Many aspiring entrepreneurs seeking to start a Non-Profit embark on this project with the wrong mindset. While nonprofits are for charitable causes, they are not "charity cases!" Non-Profit organizations are a BUSINESS.

We must first change the narrative as it relates to what a Non-Profit is in order to run it in the way it needs to be run to reap the benefits it uniquely offers due to its charitable cause. I truly believe this is caused by the "first generation entrepreneur" curse. Many grassroots nonprofit founders from the Black and Brown communities did not grow up in homes with entrepreneurial parents. Therefore, understanding the dynamics of running a business is simply not there. You are left with a hit-and-miss approach to an entity that requires strategic planning because the alternative is just too hard to face.

Like in any other profession, one must LEARN how to do the job efficiently before starting a business. For example, a personal trainer must first become certified by studying and passing an exam before soliciting clients to help them reach their health goals as a means of earning money. A surgeon must learn medicine and an attorney the law before taking on patients and clients, correct? That is because the stakes are too high not to. The alternative would be catastrophic.

Likewise, running a nonprofit is the same as having to LEARN how to run a corporation with all its unique nuances as a Non-Profit entity.

I want you to take a mental inventory as I ask you a few questions about building your nonprofit. So, if you have been taking notes, put your pen down for a moment, and focus on the following questions. I want you to consider as you ponder on the alternative for not having the proper mindset when embarking on starting your nonprofit:

1. What void are you seeking to fill with your nonprofit?
2. How severe is the social ill you are looking to address? At a local level? A national level? An international level? (You may have to do some research to check the stats)
3. If your organization could not fulfill its mission, what would happen to those needing your nonprofit's help? What would be their alternative solution? Would that alternative solution be accessible to them?
4. Are you well-prepared to successfully run a nonprofit?

If your answers to these questions concern you, you took the correct step in purchasing this book. By the end of this book, you will be much better equipped to run your organization for longevity as the goal. Now, what I want you to do in the space allotted for you at the end of this chapter is to write down the answers above so that you consistently see and remind yourself why you must educate yourself and your team to fulfill your mission statement in real time. This book will be a wonderful resource to help you meet your goals.

Most grassroots nonprofits work in communities that need it the most, so the urgency to do it correctly is even higher. Therefore, as the founder, your sense of urgency needs to be ever-present to garner the necessary information to run your organization as a BUSINESS. In a successful business, there are processes and systems that foster the growth development, and success of leadership and volunteer staff. You cannot skip the steps to leaving a legacy. So, what does it take to build a legacy? If everyone could do it, everyone would embark on having their own nonprofit versus volunteering or donating to one.

As the visionary of an organization, you are the ultimate go-to. Now, that does not mean you do or know every element of every aspect of the various departments you have within your organization. What you do have to have is the knowledge of your community, what is needed and what is required to choose the right person or group of people for the job. Whether volunteer or staff, you must choose a good team for your vision to come to fruition. Our communities are suffering, so we no longer have the luxury of entering the Non-Profit sector without the knowledge necessary to become a sustainable charitable entity. As in any business, there is competition. For every McDonald's you see, there is a Wendy's and Burger King on the same block. This is the same concept regarding Nonprofits. Do you think your organization is the only one attempting to eradicate the same cause you are trying to do away with? Do you think your nonprofit is the only one that is applying for that grant? Do you think your nonprofit is the only one soliciting funds on social media? Lastly, do you think your organization is structured in a way that would and should attain what it is you are asking for? Or is the competition more equipped? Make no mistake about it, St Jude's, ASPCA, Big Brothers Big Sisters of America ARE your competition.

When you have the mindset of an entrepreneur running a Non-Profit, your nonprofit cannot and will not go wrong. A business is a business! Non-Profit work is a business and should be viewed and respected as such. As a founder, if you do not see it that way, neither will your Board of Directors, staff, volunteers, or donors. Attitude reflects leadership and leadership is a forward-thinking, vision and result-based outlook with the service of others in mind. This is where your mindset needs to be to attain the results you need. What you do not want is to become the Blockbuster of nonprofits. Blockbuster saw the changes happening around it with the onset of streaming services like Netflix, Hulu, and did nothing to evolve the model from which it originated. Their outcome? They went out of business!

If you change your mindset, you change the game!

Far too often, I see new organizations putting the cart before the horse. They will have great ideas and a wonderful mission and vision, yet they lack the blueprint and structure to make it come together. We live in a society where the "show" of things matters more than the "reality" of things. You must also develop the mindset that building a legacy requires patience and planning. These steps cannot be rushed. Initially, founders must make fewer announcements and more moves. Set up your foundation and get your paperwork to set your business up for success. Many business owners promote on social media before doing the foundational legal work to set their business up, which is the set up for failure. For example, they may be raising funds for their organization with the very same name that another business owner legally owns and have a lawsuit awaiting them. Do not allow your good cause to end before it even begins.

Building a sustainable and long-lasting business requires intentionally building a strong foundation to support it. If you have the mindset of building your nonprofit as a business first and a charitable cause second, plan with these next steps in mind. Register your BUSINESS with the state where you will be headquartered, obtain your EIN, develop, and create your organization's bylaws. Then, obtain your tax-exempt status. As with every business, creating the face or brand of your organization is essential. The lack of initial brand recognition can make fundraising extremely difficult. Donations are generated much easier through the details, large or small. These are the building blocks for running an efficient organization. These are your stepping stones to run side-by-side with the long-standing, well-known nonprofits seeking the same funding sources as you are. You are not a business if you do not have receipts!

Entering the field of nonprofit with this mindset may not be the glamorous part of having a business, but it is necessary to having a business! As your organization grows, you will see how important setting the right mindset is. Many people who start nonprofits had excellent ideas, but did not start with the right mindset and, as a result, they are no longer here. If you take nothing else away from this chapter, understand that your organization is not a charity case. It is a legitimate business with a charitable cause. Do not build your business with the mindset of the “beggars can’t be choosers” mentality,” build your business with the mindset of strength, conviction, partnership, and collaboration.

Non-Profit Mindset

1. What void are you seeking to fill with your nonprofit?

____

____

____

2. How severe is the social ill you are looking to address? At a local level? A national level? An international level?

____

____

____

3. If your organization could not fulfill its mission, what would happen to those needing your nonprofits help? What would be their alternative solution? Would that alternative solution be accessible to them?

____

____

____

4. Are you well prepared to successfully run a nonprofit?

____

____

____

CHAPTER 2

The Myths of the 501c3 Tax Exempt Status

"Do not be satisfied with the stories that come before you…Unfold your own truth!"

– Asiya Nasir

"Now that we have our tax-exempt status, these grant funders will start funding us!" "That tax deduction is going to be our main selling point for donations." "We can't pay ourselves now that we are tax exempt!" "We don't have to file taxes because we are tax exempt!"

Any of these statements sound familiar? This chapter will demystify the myths associated with tax exemption so you can move forward with this journey in the nonprofit sector with the correct lens. For those contemplating nonprofit work, this will allow you to do so with an informed mind.

Myth #1: "Tax-Exempt Status Opens Every Door"

So let us take on the first myth that many have once they attain their 501c3 or the organization's tax-exempt status. Many nonprofit runners feel that once they receive tax-exempt status from the IRS, that status acts as a stamp of approval for every grant application the organization fills out. This is WRONG! That determination letter allows your organization to offer tax deductions for those who donate. What that determination letter does for a nonprofit is enable you to apply for grants, foundation funding and corporate sponsorship. Before this status, you may have been unable to sit at the table, but now, it puts you in the race to apply. So, while you want this status, this status does not guarantee automatic funding solely because you have that tax exempt status.

Every nonprofit must do its due diligence in creating the content, data, and infrastructure necessary for a grant funder to consider your organization for funding. In short, you must ensure that your house is in order before you put your organization on main street for review for funding. Do I have a program curriculum? Do I have my board of directors in place? Do I have my online presence in place? Do I have a budget for our programs? What data research has my organization completed to articulate the problem and how our programs and services can be the solution? Lastly, who do I need to collaborate with to make this a program that produces positive change and impact?

Ask yourself, ***is my house in order*?**

Myth #2: "That tax deduction is going to be our main selling point for donations."

A nonprofit with tax exempt status can offer a tax deduction for individual and corporate donors. However, there must be other cards for you to pull from to obtain funding. When I worked in corporate banking, I remember speaking to Investors Bank then COO, Domenick Cama. He had recently closed on a multimillion-dollar takeover of another bank we were to acquire. As a business developer of the bank, I asked him…how do you close on these huge deals? He said, "I'm able to close on those types of deals because I always go into it with the mindset that both parties are going to walk away feeling like they benefitted from the deal!" He continued, "I always show them what's in it for them as well." I never forgot that. In essence, he said that the deal must make sense for all parties involved, and it must benefit both parties for it to be deemed a good deal.

Your organization's ability to offer a tax deduction fits in this narrative. Their donation allows them to have a tax deduction as a benefit for them. Your organization can facilitate its programs and services, which benefits you. The community is uplifted which creates a healthier, more peaceful, and more productive community. That is the benefit to everyone! So yes, that is a strong selling point for you when sitting down with a potential donor. However, that cannot be the only play you have.

The IRS has made some recent changes regarding contributions made to a charitable organization. In the 2021 tax year, the IRS allowed individuals to deduct $300 and, for married couples filing jointly, $600 without itemizing other deductions. This is not the case in 2022! Individuals and businesses can reduce taxable income by completing Form 1040 Schedule A, which allows one to deduct a charitable donation along with "other itemized deductions.

Here are some examples of "other" itemized deductions:

1. State & local income or sales taxes
2. Real estate taxes
3. Personal property taxes
4. Mortgage Interest

Offering a tax deduction is a great selling point when asking for donations, so let us educate ourselves on the subject so we can provide a more educated conversation with those seeking a tax deduction in making a charitable donation to your organization. Before we do so, I do want to make this disclaimer...I would NOT initiate this conversation. This information is handy if a potential donor asks, and I would go so far as to say this if they do ask, "As I am not a tax professional, I would recommend speaking to your tax advisor to answer questions specific to your tax situation."

A great deal goes into taxes, so I would stay clear from that conversation. This is good information that should encourage you to build relationships with accountants and financial advisors. Many believe they can deduct the entire amount donated, but that is not the case. Cash donations to a public charitable organization can generally deduct up to 60% of their adjusted gross income and 30% for non-cash donations, i.e., in kind donations such as clothes, furniture and even a vehicle.

Charitable donations of $250 or more requires a written acknowledgment from your organization to claim on their tax returns. If you have not done so in the past for your donors or repeat donors, I have provided a sample of a donation letter that you can review and create your own. This is where your Tax ID number comes in. They will need that number for their accountant to complete the deduction.

If you are looking for larger donations for those needing a tax deduction, seeking individuals who would like to make a qualified charitable distribution from their IRA would be a good look for an organization. The reason is that the IRS allows an individual to contribute up to $100,000 individually to a nonprofit and, if married, both spouses can donate up to $100,000 each. It would be an excellent idea to nurture relationships with repeat donors and financial advisors and accountants.

In the past years, the IRS has changed tax deductions and charitable donations. While I would always use tax deductions as a selling point to donors, it would not be my main selling point. For some this may pose no benefit, so you need to develop and market other compelling reasons for someone to feel inspired to donate to your organization.

September 30, 2019

Dear [redacted],

Thank you for your recent generous donation of $250.00 to [redacted]. Your commitment to helping teen girls and women in our community weather the tests/obstacles in their lives is appreciated by those who help them and, most importantly, by those who benefit from our services – the girls and women of [redacted].

Thanks to donors like you, [redacted] has provided over 1000 teen girls and women with a place to feel empowered, live their dreams, learn how to overcome obstacles, and feel safe.

Your donation is being used to fund the upcoming Empowerment retreat our young girls and women participate in annually. The teen girls and women are eager to draw closer to their creator and their fellow sisters in the program. The [redacted] program, Empowerment Series and community empowerment days are designed to uplift and empower our girls/women; thus, the community.

We invite you to consider if you have not done so already in becoming a friend of our organization by completing our Recurring Donation form. We also encourage you to stop in during our weekly classes in NJ or one of our chapters in Philadelphia and Delaware and meet the young girls/women that are the recipients of your generosity. We are always open to having them meet their supporters. Please let us know when you are available.

I am always available to answer any questions you may have. Please do not hesitate to call at [redacted], or email me at [redacted]. Please note, that due to our organization being recognized as a 501c3 Tax Exempt organization; donations are tax deductible. Our Tax ID number is [redacted]

Meanwhile, we will keep you updated on the teen girls and women of our upcoming events through our social media pages and monthly emails/newsletter and website.

Again, thank you for all you do for our organization and may God accept and reward your good deed and place this in your scales of good.

Sincerely,

Executive Director/Founder

Myth #3 & 4: "We can't pay ourselves now that we are tax exempt!" and "We don't have to file taxes because we are tax exempt!"

Number 3 is truly a myth of which we will discuss more in detail in Chapter 9. So, let us address myth number four. Once you receive your determination letter indicating that the IRS recognizes you as a tax-exempt Non-Profit organization, this does not mean you do not have to file tax returns for your nonprofit each year. In fact, if you neglect to do so after three years, the IRS will revoke your tax-exempt status. So, you can understand this is serious business. Did I mention that running a nonprofit is a BUSINESS?

While the forms and the nuances of tax returns may differ from a for-profit business, EVERY nonprofit organization must complete one each year. The IRS has broken it down into two different tax returns for nonprofits. The IRS requires the first tax return from any nonprofit that has made LESS than $50,000 for the tax year. Even if you made $0 for the year, you are ***required*** to file a tax return. This tax return is called the 990EZ form. This requires you to certify with a signature that you have made less than $50,000 for the tax year. So, whether you made $0 or $49,999.99, the 990-EZ tax return must be filed to certify your income for the year. Will you have to pay taxes? No, you are tax-exempt.

The second tax return the IRS requires of nonprofits concerns any organization that makes $50,000.01 or more. This tax return is called a 990-tax return of which you must itemize the money the organization has made. This includes fundraisers, grants, donations, and in-kind donations. You must also itemize expenses, including salaries, other operational expenses, professional fees, etc. I would not recommend anyone attempting to file this on their own. This should be done with an accountant with special training in nonprofit filings. If this is not done correctly, you could be asking for an IRS audit.

There is verbiage you may not be accustomed to, so do yourself and the organization a favor and attain a professional to handle it. This is where the treasurer of your organization plays an important role. Keeping good financial records will assist the accountant tremendously when filing the tax return. This is not a sure way to avoid an audit, but it helps. Your accountant may even do a self-audit once a year to ensure your bookkeeping is impeccable for an actual audit from the IRS.

This also helps the IRS ensure that for-profit business revenue is not the primary source of income for the organization while receiving tax exempt status. This is all to make sure the organizations it provides the privilege of having that status crosses all its T's and dots all its I's. Unfortunately, some have conducted for-profit business primarily while having tax exempt status called "Unrelated Business Income." The IRS is so diligent in ensuring those of tax-exempt status are nonprofit organizations. The definition the IRS gives as it relates to Unrelated Business Income is "income from a trade or business that is regularly carried on by an exempt organization and that is not substantially related to the performance by the organization of its exempt purpose or function, except that the organization uses the profits derived from this activity." If you are wondering if you fall in that category, here are some examples of what a for-profit business receiving unrelated business income under the umbrella of a nonprofit looks like:

1. Car Dealership
2. Convenience store
3. Clothing store

These examples are different from a for-profit business recognized as a social enterprise. Please look up social enterprise, and you will see the difference. If you consistently receive funds from unrelated business income, you may need to reconsider your nonprofit entity before the IRS does it for you.

Regardless of the amount earned or donated, you must file tax returns each year as a tax-exempt nonprofit organization.

CHAPTER 3

Creating and Building Upon a Winning Board of Directors

"We must remember that one determined person can make a significant difference, and that small group of determined people can change the course of history."

– Sonia Johnson

Volunteer vs Board Member! I want you to think about that as it relates to your current board of directors, and at the end of this chapter, I will connect the dots for you. If you do not have a board yet, I want you to think about this statement based on who you envision being on your board. Why am I asking you to think about this in both scenarios? Because, in many cases, when you find an ineffective board, it is largely due to having the wrong individuals on your board of directors. Ask yourself, what are your expectations of a board member? Below, take time to consider and list your top expectations and priorities for ideal board members:

1. ____

2. ____

3. ____

4. ____

5. ____

6. ____

7. ____

8. ____

9. ____

10. ____

Does any of this look familiar to what you wrote?

1. Passion for the mission
2. Love of community

3. Supportive, like my best friend, he/she supports anything I do
4. Wants the organization to succeed
5. Show up to meetings, events, and fundraisers
6. Provides constructive and valuable feedback

If this list looks like some of the expectations you wrote, that is because these are the most common expectations that new founders or existing founders of struggling organizations require. Don't feel bad! When I began my nonprofit J.E.S.S.I.C.A. Cares twelve years ago, I shared those same expectations. While these are good expectations, they do not provide clarity to the potential board member or you as the leader as to what that looks like in "real time" and due to that, you never achieve the goals you have set for your organization and simply put, these expectations are not enough. You see, wanting the organization to succeed may look different to you then to your board member(s), so, as the visionary of the Non-Profit, you have to breakdown what that looks like to assess if the person you are considering has those qualifications and then articulate those expectations in a way where the potential board member can see themselves in that position. You cannot assume that when you give the expectations mentioned on your list, the vision is interpreted in the same way.

While some of these expectations are nice, they are not enough to bring to fruition the organization's mission or the success. That may be the vision overall, but you must provide details of what your ideal potential board member looks like to achieve your end goal. In the next few pages, we will review specific expectations that are necessary in your search to attain an efficient and "winning" board. This chapter is one of the book's most important chapters due to the level of importance you see and hold your board of directors to.

Expectation #1: Adherence to the board governance (Bylaws)

Adherence to your organization's bylaws is extremely important. The bylaws are the "code of conduct" of your organization. The bylaws should cover attendance, member term, conflict of interest, voting system, frequency of meetings i.e., monthly, quarterly, etc. When assessing who you would like to have on your board, is this an individual who follows protocol, or are they known for the opposite? Is this an individual who will encourage new board members to adhere to the bylaws by example? Without adherence to the bylaws, the board meetings will be chaotic at the very least. Why? Because there needs to be a protocol as to who the chair of the board is, their role, the voting system, how decisions are made for the organization, and the list goes on. I am a firm believer in people staying in their lane. If you have board officers, are they doing their job efficiently? When the board members stay in their lane, as the late Nipsey Hussle said, "there's no traffic in your lane." Therefore, there is no discord. While there may be differences of opinion from time to time which I encourage, those conversations can be had professionally due to the bylaws being adhered to with the understanding that no one is above the bylaws.

So, when discussing with someone who you believe may be a good fit, presenting and discussing the bylaws may be a good practice because if they disagree with what is in the bylaws it would be better to find that out in the initial conversation then to have them on the board and now it has become a disruption to the growth and flow of the organization.

Ensure this is the first expectation they understand is a requirement for a successful and cohesive board. Their buy-in or lack thereof, will be a good indicator of, will this be a good fit?

Expectation #2 Funding Sources/Annual Requirement

As the Founder, you should not be the only individual searching for funding sources to further the organization's mission. One of the major expectations you should have with your board of directors is that they understand they are responsible for bringing in funding sources. For example, each board of director should have a specific dollar amount they need to donate or raise for the organization each year. Why should this be a requirement? Well, there are several reasons. The first reason is that, as board of directors, they are ambassadors for the organization, meaning they will ask for donations from others. Nothing shows integrity like putting your money where your mouth is. A board of director can advocate better when asking for donations when they can say to a potential funder, "I donate towards __________ because I believe in the cause, so not only do I donate my time as a board member, I am also a donor." That personal touch and explanation when speaking to someone on the fence can be compelling.

The second reason why having a board member donate towards the mission it serves is that it ensures recurring expenses are paid, i.e., supplies, website hosting, accounting services, etc. Let me show you an example, say you have seven board members. Each board member is required to bring in $1,500 annually. Now let me be clear, the board member can monetarily support from their personal funds to meet this annual requirement or ask friends, and colleagues, to support. Say each board member of this seven-member team brought in $1,500, you would have $10,500. Now ask yourself, what could my nonprofit do with $10,500.00? Fund a program or an event?

If a board member scoffs at supporting the organization in this capacity, what do you think they would do when asked to support a campaign or fundraiser? This reflects their attitude towards the cause and that they do not see the sense of urgency regarding the cause you seek to champion. Now, this could be an opportunity to further educate the board member or a moment of clarity to see if this is a good fit.

This is the expectation many founders find very difficult to ask of their board members, but successful Non-Profits all do, which is a key factor in having a successful board. Grant funding and fundraisers do not always come through, so an organization should have a Plan. This should be one of them.

Expectation #3 Resources & Expertise

A nonprofit organization requires individual donors, volunteers, companies, and grant funders to lend what they can to contribute to the success of evoking change for a particular cause or mission. When choosing a potential board member, consider what this individual can "lend" to the organization. Does this potential board member possess connections to your intended community? Why is this important? Because as a nonprofit, your board of directors should be a source of providing opportunities that will benefit the organization. That can be in the form of an introduction to a CEO, CFO, or community relations person. These types of resources can be at your disposal **IF** you articulate to your board that this is important to the success and sustainability of the organization. Who you do not know, your board member may know!

When selecting your ideal team of board members, you expect they will bring expertise to the table. Let us take an accountant as an example. This accountant may offer bookkeeping, filing your annual tax return for free, or provide you with self-audits to ensure your financial records are above reproach. An accountant can also introduce you to some of their colleagues. You may be asking yourself, why is that important? During tax season, and, throughout the year, as they help clients, some of those clients may need a tax deduction---what better way for an accountant to assist a client than by offering a solution? Your organization may be that solution. The better the relationship you build with the accountant, the more likely you will receive a contribution in exchange for a tax deduction. Having an accountant who can perform a dual role, can extend their expertise and the resources that contributes to the organization.

As another example, a business attorney would also lend their expertise to your board of directors. When handling contracts with collaborators or venues, contract law expertise can save the organization a lot of headaches. The same can be applied to someone having an expertise in web design, web hosting, graphic design, and more. This is not to say that you cannot obtain this within your volunteer pool, but a board member with a certain skill set can advance the organization while saving money.

Expectation #4 Being a Spokesperson/Ambassador

As a board of directors' member, these individuals are the decision makers. They are the ones that guide the vision. Those that sit on the board have passion for the mission. They believe in the cause, make decisions, and commit to ensuring that that vision comes to fruition. With that being said, it should be an expectation that in appropriate settings, a board member should mention that they are on the board of a charitable organization and bring awareness to the mission and the issue the organization is looking to address.

Let's take apart the word's "ambassador" or "spokesperson." The definition of an ambassador is "a person who acts as a representative or promoter of a specified activity." Now let us look at what the definition is of a spokesperson. A spokesperson is "a person who is chosen to speak officially for a group or organization." Would you say that is what you would expect from a board member? Someone chosen to speak on behalf of the organization; meaning, at networking events, to colleagues and friends to bring an awareness to a fundraiser or your cause? I love how the word ambassador means a "promoter" of a specified activity, organization, or person. If your board of directors believe in the mission, they are stewards of the organization.

This can be demonstrated in many ways, such as promoting upcoming events, sending invitations to open houses and fundraisers on their social media pages, sharing with their colleagues at work and wearing apparel that promotes your organization so that it evokes conversation. These are some of the ways in which one can be an ambassador for the organization. Another way is if the founder or executive director cannot attend an event as a representative of the organization, then stepping in and filling those duties to speak to those in attendance about the organization would be a perfect example.

If you ask a board member to do any one of these things and they take issue with doing so, this may be a sign that you need to have a conversation about the role and purpose of a board member.

Expectation #5 Recruiter of future Board Members

People associate themselves with like-minded individuals. Have you ever heard that if you surround yourself with ten successful individuals, you will be the eleventh? Or contrary to that, if you surround yourself with ten individuals who are not productive, then you will be the eleventh? Think about this as it relates to your board members and their ability to recruit future board members. As we know and should be practicing, Non-Profit board members should have a maximum term with an organization. As that time approaches, organizations must discuss who will replace that board member.

What better way than to have a current board member who knows the ins and outs of the organization, expectations, goals, and needs to make an introduction to like-minded people to increase the compatibility between your organization and the new board member?

By having the board of directors reach out to them to obtain what you can call a "feeler" and inform the potential new board member that they were hand-selected to become a board member, this makes an individual feel honored and eager to reciprocate. Even if it is not a good fit, you have done the introduction in such a way that that individual may recommend someone or be a potential candidate to revisit the opportunity at a later time.

Again, with expectations of being a board member in place, it helps everyone understand what it takes for a successful active, participating team to run as efficiently as possible.

Expectation #6 Chairing A Committee

As a nonprofit, you will need to create committees to be responsible for the important aspects of running a Non-Profit, i.e., committees devoted to fundraising, finance, and volunteering. These are important areas in growing the organization and should not be left to one individual. As board members, they are in a leadership role and have direct access to what the organization is doing. As mentioned earlier in this chapter, they may have an expertise that makes them a competent chairperson for a particular committee.

Committees are there to focus on one thing or area. For example, the fundraising committee should be focused solely on creating effective fundraisers that will financially benefit the organization. A board member will know what the program budget is for a particular program and have the annual budget, so this will help the committee tremendously as it relates to how much they need to raise per fundraiser as a goal. A chairperson is the go between from the board to the committee. This eliminates delays in getting things approved.

Having designated duties and responsibilities for certain board members and committees is important for several reasons:

1. It allows the founder and executive director more time to complete their own responsibilities
2. It allows the board member to serve the organization in a capacity that aligns with their skills/talents
3. This creates succession planning for the organization. For example, the board member is acting as a self-starter under the nonprofit's umbrella. Perhaps teaching a volunteer the role of the board member, which is a position that volunteer may aspire to in the future.

There are great benefits to challenging your board to rise to the occasion. Everyone wins. The organization wins. The individual wins. The recipients of your organization win. Through delegation, you build up a process and chain of command which streamlines the process of getting things done efficiently. This is due in part because no one individual is being taxed.

This goes back to my original statement at the onset of this chapter… ***"Volunteer vs Board Member."*** In looking at some of these fundamental expectations, when choosing a potential board member, ask yourself, does this individual possess these qualities, abilities, skill sets, and connections to influence change and action? Are they leaders in their own right? You MUST ask the questions because, far too often, when you do not, you end up with volunteers in board member positions. Now don't get me wrong. Volunteers are the soul of nonprofits and play a tremendous role. However, their job description requires very different skill sets. Far too often, due to the founder's lack of confidence, they will ask friends and family and while they may have good intentions, they lack the experience or connections to the community to evoke real change.

I have learned throughout the years of consulting with new founders and existing founders who are struggling that they know what they want from their board members, but are too intimidated to ask those who possess the qualities, connections, and skill sets they need. They may think, "I have this small nonprofit, so this person wouldn't want to be a part of my board" or "we don't have everything together yet, but once we do, I'll feel confident to ask." This type of thinking is what holds them back. If you do not have the team necessary to propel you to the next level, you will never have "everything together" to finally have the confidence to ask the right people to be on your team.

That IS the selling point when speaking to individuals of influence and leadership. If they believe in your cause, they will be happy to lend their resources, expertise, and time to champion your cause with you. Ask yourself, if my organization fails to deliver the mission to our target audience, what is their alternative? If the alternative is too hard to bear, that should be your motivation and selling point to the individual you feel you are not ready to ask. Share with them that you know they have what it takes to truly make a difference within the organization and community.

If you do not believe enough in your cause, how do you expect anyone else to? Get your head in the game. Remember, a nonprofit's mission should always be greater than the fear.

CHAPTER 4

The Heart of Your Non-Profit: Volunteers

"Volunteering is at the very core of being a human! No one has made it through life without someone else's help!"

– Heather French Henry

Let's talk facts. Without volunteers, nonprofits would not be able to serve the community as they do. Volunteers are the heart of any nonprofit and should be held in high esteem. What is so unique about volunteers is that they truly give their time, expertise, and sometimes even donations because they genuinely believe in the cause. Their biggest reward is seeing their services render someone happier.

In my consulting journey, many of my clients indicate that one of the main reasons they struggle is that they do not have the support to do all the necessary things related to the workforce. Simply put, there needs to be more volunteers. I challenge my clients to examine that statement. According to Volunteering and Civic Life in America/AmeriCorps, an estimated 23.2 percent of Americans or more than 60.7 million formally volunteered with organizations between September 2020 and 2021. In total, these volunteers served an estimated 4.1 billion hours with an economic value of $122.9 billion.

One of the nonprofit organization's successes is managing its volunteers. According to statistics, the volunteers ARE there to manage. Therefore, in the following pages, we will cover the most efficient way to manage a group of passionate individuals looking to support your cause for FREE.

Volunteer Management #1 Assign a Chairperson

Nonprofit organizations are pretty good at soliciting volunteers. The issue comes with retaining volunteers. The main reason why this happens is that this group of talented, passionate individuals gets lost in the shuffle of an organization. When a volunteer feels like they are not valued, they tend to find another organization that makes them feel needed and appreciated. One of the worst things that can happen to a willing and ready volunteer is they show up ready to work, and there either is no work, direction, or leadership. Without these key elements, volunteers will lose initiative and interest.

One way to avoid that is by assigning a committee chair. For this conversation, a Volunteer Committee Chairperson is someone who can advocate for the volunteers within your organization. A nonprofit should choose a chairperson as one of the board members because as mentioned previously, there is a direct link from the committee to decision making. The board member can relay all questions, issues, concerns, and recommendations to the board promptly. A committee chairperson can do much to ensure the efficiency of the volunteers. For example, they can lead the effort of creating a welcoming process for each new volunteer. A committee chairperson can ensure regular meetings within the volunteer committee to keep the volunteers in a constant state of "in the know," which is vital to a volunteer's support.

A volunteer chairperson can send out reminders and sign -up sheets for upcoming events to attend and assist. This also creates a chain of command, allowing the executive director the free time to handle more pressing matters that can impact the organization. A volunteer chairperson can also see when an issue is arising and nip it in the bud quickly. This form of leadership helps the organization and it helps the chairperson sharpen their leadership skills. It also ensures things run smoothly for the recipients looking to benefit from your services.

Volunteer Management #2 Create a VRM system for your volunteers

In sales, a customer relationship management system (CRM) gathers a customer's information. In the nonprofit world, we could us a similar model to gather a volunteer's personal information. A volunteer relationship management (VRM) system would help retain volunteer's personal information and help you nurture relationships with your volunteers. In this software, it gathers a volunteer's information such as the following:

1. Contact Information (e.g., name, address, phone number)
2. Volunteer Hours (e.g., part-time, full-time, etc.)
3. Skill sets, expertise
4. Languages
5. Hobbies
6. Motivations and goals
7. Family information (e.g., marital status, anniversaries, birthdates, children)
8. Work status (e.g., full-time, part-time, retired)
9. Past experiences with other Non-Profits

You may be asking yourself, why do I need to collect this type of information on my volunteers? It is one thing to attract them, it's another thing to retain them. There needs to be a system in place to streamline the process for an organization to tap into showing appreciation and recognizing above and beyond service work. A VRM system can aid your organization in remembering important dates and events regarding your volunteers such as anniversaries, birthdays, etc. When a volunteer feels valued, they will be more loyal, more easily lend their expertise and services, be a proud ambassador of the organization, and more. Successful businesses are known for the process and systems they put in place for their companies. Does your organization deserve less? Is it not a business also?

Volunteer Management #3 Create A Calendar of Upcoming Events

At each volunteer committee meeting, this calendar should be present. Whether a virtual calendar or a desk-size calendar. You need to be on the same page regarding scheduling. The reason for this is so that you can manage the dates and times that volunteers said they would serve at those events. If circumstances have changed for some, then your organization can be proactive in ensuring that someone else can step in their place. This makes for a stress-free event and committee of volunteers. When individuals work in a stress-free environment, their lack of stress will be evident to those around them and those they interact with.

Volunteer Management #4 Potential Board Members

As with every board of directors, their term of service will end. Your pool of volunteers may be a great source to pull from to replace those leaving, granted they have the ability, time commitment, etc., to fulfill the obligations of a board member. This is a great point position to explore for new board members because of the following reasons:

1. Existing commitment to the mission and organization
2. Work ethics and demonstration of leadership
3. Familiarity with the existing board of directors

For these reasons, if you take care of your team of volunteers, they will take care of your organization and its recipients. Proper management is key. Remember, this is a special group of individuals. You cannot incentivize them with pay, but by leading with a clear intention of leading with a cause to champion, and that all play a part in making that happen, you end up with a win-win situation every time.

Bonus: The next page will have a Volunteer Application sample. Use this with anyone interested in being part of your organization. You will see why in the next chapter.

YOUR LOGO HERE

VOLUNTEER APPLICATION

Application can be submitted one of two ways:

a. **Filled out and hand delivered at a ██████████ event**

b. **Filled out and emailed to** jessica@jessicacares.org

Name: ____

Address: ____

____

Home/Mobile Phone#: ________________________________

Email Address: _____________________________________

Number of Hours Available To Volunteer Each Week: (Please Circle)
❖ **1-5 Hours:** ❖ **5-10 Hours:** ❖ **10-20 Hours:**

Please list the time frames you are available to volunteer during the week or on weekends:

Monday	**Start:**		**End:**		**Friday**	**Start:**		**End:**	
Tuesday	**Start:**		**End:**		**Saturday**	**Start:**		**End:**	
Wednesday	**Start:**		**End:**		**Sunday**	**Start:**		**End:**	
Thursday	**Start:**		**End:**						

List Any Previous or Current Volunteer Experience:		
Organization	**Position/Major Responsibility**	**Dates of Service (mm/yy) From: To:**

Position(s) Volunteering For: (Circle the Applicable)
❖ **Office/Admin Support** ❖ **Social Media/Marketing** ❖ **Website Maintenance** ❖ **Graphic Design** ❖ **Photography** ❖ **Youth Mentoring** ❖ **Event Planning** ❖ **Fundraising Development** ❖ **Leadership Development** ❖ **Volunteer Coordination**

Are you willing to take a background check? Yes ☐ No ☐

How did you hear about this opportunity? (Please Circle)

1. **Social Media (Instagram, Facebook, Twitter)**
2. **Internet Search**
3. **Family/Friend**

CHAPTER 5

Creating a Corporate Culture as A Charitable Organization

"Integrity is the most valuable and respected quality of leadership. Always keep your word!

– Brian Tracy

Attitude reflects leadership! When you think of the work environment you would like your organization to provide to its board of directors, volunteers, and recipients…what does that look like? This is crucial, especially in the Non-Profit sector, because you are mainly dealing with non-paid individuals. Your environment will play a huge factor in their returning over and over again in the capacity to serve.

We can all remember a job or supervisor we worked for in the past that did not create a workplace environment that promoted growth, support, creativity, or productivity. Those were the jobs that, even with pay, we would have rather been anywhere else. Imagine if it were on a voluntary basis. Would you have gone back? I am sure the answer is with a resounding NO. So, what makes you think if not intentional with the positive corporate culture you want to create, your board of directors and volunteers won't decide to do the same? I think you would agree that the intention must be there and what that looks like for all parties involved must be made crystal clear. With anything that you want to change, you must start within FIRST. So, if the goal is to empower the community or a certain group of individuals, then you have to lead by example so that others will have a blueprint to implement themselves. This requires you, as the founder or aspiring founder, to have some core values and what I call the three C's of corporate culture.

Let us start with you and what core values you must possess to be intentional about the culture you want to create within your organization. Below, list five of your non-negotiable core values:

1. ______________________________

2. ______________________________

3. ______________________________

4. ______________________________

5. ____

Examine your five core values and ask yourself; do I exemplify that each day? Am I intentional with my core values when interacting with others? Am I known for these core values? Do I act consistently with my values? These are important and necessary questions to ask because, for you to create this for your organization, it must be something you embody as the visionary for others to emulate for your nonprofit.

When something is a part of you as it relates to integrity, it will be consistent; not contingent on a mood or anything external, which we know can change from day to day. Integrity is defined as "the quality of being honest and having strong moral principles that you refuse to change!" This should be the cornerstone of your leadership because it sets the tone for everyone else who is a part of your team and any potential staff, board, or volunteers to understand this "culture" is non-negotiable.

Leadership within your organization must take an active role in defining the "corporate culture" of your charitable organization. That starts with being very clear as to why your organization even exists. The why must be the motivating factor, the influencer, and the thing that you live by. Your non-profit organization is and will be your legacy, long after you are gone. What do you want your organization to be remembered for?

Let us start with the 3 C's of creating a corporate culture within your nonprofit. Those three C's are "***communication, connection and celebration***." While this is the foundation, we will discuss some other factors in this chapter.

Communication

For there to be a culture, everyone must be on the same page and have the same understanding. The organization's mission should be communicated thoroughly regardless of the individual's capacity within the nonprofit. If you have a board of directors, do they know the mission statement? The purpose of your organization? Do they know why you started the nonprofit? Do they know what the alternative is without your organization's help to the community? This should be communicated often and from the beginning.

Communicating to your volunteers will motivate them to keep coming and to provide service to those you have committed to serving because they understand what faces those who seek your assistance. They understand the odds stacked against them. Therefore, that passion and sense of urgency will always be present in every individual who is attached to your organization. Often, people in need are continuously made to feel ashamed. This should not be with your organization. Your organization is there to provide hope so that sentiment should be felt and expressed by everyone. It needs to be part of the organization's culture.

Here are some helpful tips to assist you in communicating in an impactful way within your organization:

1. When recruiting board members, mention your mission statement and then **provide** the potential member with a clear understanding of why you exist, the impact your organization can make given the right people are involved, a history of why you got started, and the development stages you have accomplished since inception.

2. Complete this step with each volunteer as well. This should be done on a biannual basis so new volunteers can have the opportunity to learn about the organization.

3. At the top of the itinerary for board or volunteer meetings, you should clearly express the organization's mission statement. Statistics show that it takes seven touches for something to stick, so if you are meeting monthly and you start each meeting with the reading of the mission statement, it will help everyone assess themselves and the organization with one question in mind. Are we living the mission? At these meetings, communicating the importance of making each recipient of your services feel like they left better than how they came should be of utmost importance.

This level of communication will ensure that all parties are on the same page and championing your cause.

Connection

When we are connected to something, we are more indebted to it. It becomes something we hold dear. This holds for the mission of your nonprofit. Ensure those who want to be a part of your work are connected. I remember when I first embarked on nonprofit work on a high level because the corporate job I had at the time made it a requirement for my employment. While I had supported nonprofits before, now it was on a higher level, and if I am being honest, it was not out of the kindness of my heart. It was an obligation that eventually became something I felt strongly connected to.

When those who are interested in serving on the board or as a volunteer, ask them THEIR why. Why do they want to serve in that capacity? What do they feel they can bring to the organization? After communicating the things mentioned in the previous pages, ask them what impact do they want to make while servicing your organization. Now you can assess their connection to your cause and those who benefit from your cause. Is it stemming from a personal experience?

That is why sharing why you started your nonprofit is essential to building that connection. Two things can happen: either the other person shares in a similar way, which drew them to your work or they are now drawn by your story even more. Either way, the connection, bond, and loyalty are now on a new level.

This is creating a culture of commitment grounded in commonality from the founder to everyone coming to join you and a desire to make a difference. Here are some tips to help you keep your team connected:

1. Challenge them to share their ideas with the organization and make it a point to utilize them as often as you can, even if you must adjust some areas. This allows everyone to see in real-time that they are contributing to the eradication of the cause you are fighting for.
2. Have them share beautiful interactions with the recipients at meetings. Everyone loves a success story or happy ending, so share these stories at meetings. This allows everyone to hear the impact of those that are receiving help. There is no better way to stay connected then hearing the testimonials of those you help.
3. Send quarterly surveys to board members and volunteers, asking them how they feel about the organization. Do they feel heard? Do they see the impact of the organization? This allows you to make improvements timelier, engage better, and implement effectively.

Celebrate

Celebrate those who celebrate your mission! Good begets good. You can never celebrate your team enough. When you feel appreciated, it makes you want to do more. An individual's success should be celebrated as the entire team's success due to the efforts of one person stepping up and giving of themselves. Here are some tips on ways you can recognize good work:

1. Select a Board Member or Volunteer of the Month
2. Host an Annual Team Recognition Dinner
3. Spotlight a donor or volunteer on the organization's website or newsletter
4. Host a lunch with the Founder
5. Write a handwritten letter expressing gratitude
6. Develop fun teambuilding workshops

This does not have to be initiated by you as the Founder alone. This is something that the entire board of directors can take on. Again, creating a corporate culture requires the leadership to take an active role in defining that culture.

CHAPTER 6

Does Anyone Know Your Story?

"Storytelling offers the opportunity to talk with your audience, not at them!"

Unlike a for-profit business, nonprofits do not sell a product for a cost that turns into profit. Instead, nonprofits "sell" a nontangible service where the donor is left with the feeling of helping someone else and doing something for the greater good. It provides an emotional satisfaction that yields the same sentiment. I would even go so far as to say it yields a better feeling than receiving an item for purchase. For-profit enterprises typically tell their "story" by displaying the item on individuals who look good in their product so you can see yourself wearing, driving, vacationing, and eating anything they display. That is their story.

Not true with nonprofit storytelling. This form of marketing looks different and is crucial to the organization's stability. Attracting donors requires a distinct marketing strategy and storytelling plays a tremendous role in accomplishing that strategy. Donors, whether individual, corporate, foundation or grant funders need to know the who, what, where, and why to evoke what is necessary to make that donation, contribution, or sponsorship. Here is what I mean:

1. **Who**: Those looking to support you need to know two points of reference related to the "who." Who you are helping? Is your organization advocating for youth? Is this geared toward senior citizens? Male, female? Then the other who is "who" are you as a nonprofit? Who is the Founder? Who are your board members?

This helps to make that introduction. You are making that introduction with the "who."

2. **What**: This is where you share your story of what you do as an organization and provide your mission statement as a story. This would include what services you provide to champion your cause. This would include your programs, and resources.

3. **Where**: This allows donors to know where you provide your services. This helps recipients, as well. If the services you provide are within distance of their location, it provides them hope. This also allows you to research "community" grants specific to your mission AND location. Those grants are only given to those within the community. This also helps those seeking to volunteer near to their location.
4. **Why**: This is the most important part of telling your story. This establishes what the alternative is without your organization. Non-Profits fill a void in the community, and you must explain how your organization will fill that void. This is where you use statistics and facts to support your cause. You basically take the blinders off for many to see how devastating a matter truly is. This evokes emotion coupled with the logic of the epidemic you are trying to eradicate. By the way, this is grant writing 101.

This is your story and you can tell it in whatever fashion you want to tell it. You can do so with a documentary, showing those you are seeking to help, having experts in the documentary share the facts, and then displaying the works that your organization is doing to change that narrative. You may be thinking to yourself, you may not have the funds to create a documentary and that may be true. What you do have is a smartphone that can create and share stories to "sell" your organization as one everyone wants to support.

Think of the best nonprofit storytellers right now. St. Jude's shares the "who," - their pediatric cancer patients and their families, the "what" which is the services they provide at NO cost to the families, the "where," are the locations and the housing they provide for the families during treatment, and the "why," which is so no child will be turned down due to the lack of the parents' ability to pay medical expenses or lack of medical coverage. They share the statistics of children who die each year from the deadly disease and how many children they have helped. This is so those tuning in can see in real-time the impact their donation or volunteer support will do. ASPCA functions similarly with animals.

Now, there are FREE methods to sharing your story. You can share your story across social media and account subscriptions. This is brilliant because the more subscribers you have and notifications to the channel, the more you are connecting those who can help with those who need their help. Social media, whether through YouTube, Instagram, or TikTok, will share your message and connect to others. You can share information, create viral videos, answer questions easily, and so on. You have TikTok now which captures a younger audience who are truly savvy in sharing to various platforms, exposing you to new supporters. This is your opportunity to share your nonprofit story. You have the power to share your story in whatever way you like with an immediate audience.

Ask yourself…does anyone KNOW our story? Do people truly know who we help, who we are, what we do, and why we do it? If you cannot say YES, then you have not been sharing your story enough. Be clear about where their contributions will go. Is a certain dollar amount going to sponsor one individual or more? What services and programs will directly impact the recipients? What will happen without their generous donations? Create that happy ending with them being a part of it.

I would like to share a few statistics so that you can see that there are donors out there looking for a nonprofit to support. During the height of Covid, look at the staggering numbers of those who contributed in 2020 alone:

1. **449 billion dollars was donated**

2. **Corporate Giving (Businesses): 5% ($22,450 Million)**
3. **Grant Money: 9% ($40,410 Million)**
4. **Foundations: 17% ($763,300 Million)**
5. **Individual Donations: 69% (3 plus Billion)**

As you can see, donors are waiting to support you. If not you, it will be another Non-Profit organization benefitting from their generosity. Yes, you have competition. Always keep in mind your charitable story is connected to someone's cry for help. Individuals, companies, and grant funders cannot support an organization they do not know exists. Your main objective in telling your story is to raise the consciousness and realization of a matter. Therefore, create your story, gather the players, and TELL your story. On the next page you will find a worksheet that can assist you in developing the blueprint of your story.

Who: Who is the subject of the story? Who is the protagonist in your story? Is this a recipient of your services? A Board Member? A Volunteer?

____

____

What: What story do you want to tell? The history of the organization? The journey of one of your recipients? What was the beginning, the middle and then end? What is the happy ending? What social ill are you trying to eradicate? What is your call to action? (Donations, corporate sponsorship, recruiting for donors, volunteers?

____

____

Where: Where do you offer your services? What underserved community are you serving? Where can they find you? (Online presence, e.g., social media, Website)

____

____

Why: Why did you start your organization? What is the why in your purpose?

____

____

CHAPTER 7

Think Outside the Box: Secure the Funds

"If you need to raise funds from donors, you need to study them, respect them, and build everything you do around them."

– Jeff Brooks

Nonprofit fundraising will feel like a never-ending cycle. As I have mentioned, your primary financial source is donations, whether individuals, grants, or corporate sponsorship. It is necessary to keep your doors open, sustain your services, and build the legacy you want to create. Aside from grants and individual donations, some find it difficult to seek funding in other ways. This chapter will provide you with "outside of the box" fundraising techniques. The reality is that every grant application you apply for will NOT be approved so you must have a backup so that you do not lose momentum or experience downtime within your organization.

This is where creating your annual budget to see what you are looking at when you ask yourself, ***what would a successful year look like for my organization*** matters. And how much will that successful year cost our organization? This raises the awareness of what you must raise, earn, or be awarded in grants. This helps you decide which grants to go after and what conversations you will have amongst individuals and corporation owners regarding where the funds will go and how much.

Here are some novel new ideas to help you secure your funds. I learned about some of these tools in my corporate banking days and transferred that knowledge to make it work for my nonprofit organization. I hope it will do the same for you.

1. **Conversations and Cocktails or Mingle and Mocktails**: This is where you invite a selected few to attend a very intimate setting where you, your board members, and one or two of your recipients are in the room. No need for a big spread, just some appetizers will do, and converse with those in attendance about the organization's vision, goals, and obstacles. Introduce the key members of your team. Have the recipients share how your organization has impacted them directly and then ask for monetary donations. Have your means of accepting donations readily accessible, such as

Square, PayPal, Zelle, your website or CashApp. Make it almost impossible for someone to say NO.

2. **Accountants**: Have your board of directors create a list of accountants they know, along with their contact information, which includes their email address, phone number, and address. During tax season, create a budget for each board member to purchase "midnight snacks" that includes a basket of teas/coffee, cookies, popcorn, and small bags of chips for the accountants for the long hours they will be working. Have your team bring a handful of your brochures, which should have your Tax ID number in the "make a donation" section, and hand it to them with a small invite to mention your organization for a client needing a tax deduction. Having multiple accountants doing this can result in some sizable contributions.
3. **Financial Advisors**: You can apply this to a Financial Advisor as it relates to having your board members creating a list. Because many financial advisors cannot accept gifts, ask first if it would be okay. Regardless of the answer, take the approach of setting up a time for the founder or executive director of the organization and the Financial Advisor to speak. Talk to them about the desire for the organization's longevity, vision, and mission. Bring along brochures, as well. This is so the Financial Advisor can mention your organization to someone considering leaving some funds from their estate to a charitable cause. With IRS contributions being so attractive, they can also talk to individuals that qualify for a need in tax deductions through their IRA.
4. **Financial Institute**: If your nonprofit has a banking relationship with a financial institution, ask to meet with the

local branch manager to make an introduction to the community relations officer of the bank. When meeting with the branch manager provide them with a brochure as well so they can become acquainted with the services and programs you provide. You should also bring a one-page letter of introduction to be presented to the community relations officer. Your objective of this meeting is to secure funds by asking the bank to participate in a "Jean Day." Employees of financial institutions require a certain dress code, and jeans are not one of them. However, explore securing funds in a different way by asking for a day in which bank employees can have a dress-down day or "Jean Day." If they would like to participate, they must contribute $5 and that $5 serves as a donation to your nonprofit organization.

There are so many ideas that can take your organization to the next level regarding funding. Traditional fundraisers like Bowl-A-Thons and shirt-selling, should still be part of your fundraising strategy. However, as the saying goes, you cannot put all your eggs in one basket, so learn how to diversify your fundraising strategy to ensure sustainability.

You can encourage the fundraising committee to participate in this to see if they can generate some "out of the box" ideas for securing funding. Another effective way to accomplish "out of the box" ideas is by soliciting a fundraising specialist. Initially, your organization may not have the budget for a specialist, so the suggestions provided in this chapter can aid your organization in the interim. As you consider expansion and growth, a fundraising specialist would be a crucial component to ensuring its success in your appeal for funds.

Bonus: On the next page, the worksheet provided will guide you in developing your "out of the box" action plan.

"Out of the Box Suggestion Sheet

Suggestion #1

1.

Suggestion #2

2.

CHAPTER 8

Nurturing the Donor Relationship

"A person who feels appreciated will always do more than what is expected."

This chapter focuses on securing a good relationship with your donors. Great storytelling is the catalyst to securing the continuity of your organization. So, explore this chapter if you want to protect the continuance of your mission. Many grassroots nonprofits function from a project to project, event to event, program to program functionality. While it allows you to host events and facilitate programs from time to time, as the saying goes…when you know better, you do better.

We do not want to fundraise ONLY when a project is coming up. Successful nonprofits fundraise and solicit funds throughout the year with the ANNUAL budget in mind. Moreover, imploring individuals and businesses for each project becomes tiring and burdensome for the organization and the donor. There must be a better way. This requires a two-part game plan. We discussed the first part of it, "telling your story," and then always ending your story with a call to action, asking for a donation. So, we have the first part, and now the second part demands more intention, which is nurturing the relationship with your donors.

This requires a system in place. This should become the norm, but with a clear picture of the impact and connection it brings between donor and organization. To nurture the donor relationship is to develop a relationship with each donor in some way. The most impactful way to nurture the relationship is to:

1. Identify
2. Qualify
3. Cultivate and Nurture
4. Ask
5. Thank them

Let us break down each category so that you can see how to foster long-lasting relationships with your donors.

Identify

Create a database for your donors. Who has donated to your organization in the past? Have they donated more than once? Is it a certain amount each time? Do they engage with your organization's social media pages with support? Do they subscribe to anything that you have? Do they share the work, fundraisers, and events on their social media pages?

This is identifying the donor. Did they make large or smaller donations? This allows you to see the donor's potential because, even if small, you can then identify them as a potential "friend" of the organization that can provide a small amount consistently. You will see what I mean in the next section.

Qualify

Now that you have identified your donor(s) based on a pattern for amount and consistency, you can qualify them for certain fundraisers. For example, you may have a donor that donates $25.00 consistently. If you were to identify that, you could see the potential of that $25.00 on a monthly basis as a $300 annual contribution to your organization, you can qualify them as a "recurring donor." What could your nonprofit do with $300? Add five to ten more donors like that. Do you see the need to identify and qualify the donor relationship with you?

Cultivate-Nurture

When you want to foster a relationship, there are several ways to ensure they continue to support you. As in any relationship, communication is vital to developing a strong bond. There are several ways in which you can nourish the relationship through communication. Here are some of the ways in which you can communicate with your donors on a consistent basis:

1. A monthly newsletter, where you may want to highlight a donor to acknowledge their contributions.
2. An annual letter reflecting the total amount of their donations for the year to recognize their contributions.
3. Have them subscribe to notifications for upcoming events and fundraisers to keep them informed.
4. Phone your donors to see how they are doing and not asking for anything to provide them with personal attention.
5. Create a donor relationship management program where you can maintain important information about them, such as anniversaries with your organization and for personal care.

These constant touches with your donors will keep them connected to your cause.

<u>Ask</u>

There will be moments when your organization will find itself in a deficit. It could be because a fundraiser did not generate the expected profit or an individual pledge did not come through. This is when you send out a call for help to ask those who have bought into your cause to contribute again outside of the norm. This should not be the norm, but there is another way to nurture the relationship by communicating in this way, "Good Morning__________. This is _______________(this should be either the Executive Director or one of the Board Members). How are you doing today? (Wait for the response and then respond ACCORDINGLY). I am reaching out to a selected pool of our donors for a very special request. (Explain briefly the issue/transparency is essential). We at (name of the organization) are looking to close the deficit and while we appreciate all that you do for us, if you are able to make a special donation or know of someone who can, we would greatly appreciate it. Your donation will impact_________________________________"

Of course, you can adjust this or create a script that you and your board members can practice to make it more conversational. The point is to focus on your "relationship" with this donor. In doing so, you have created a space for special requests because you communicate often without asking. It is not burdensome for them to answer the request.

Thanking The Donors

This may sound like a given, but statistics show that people stop giving because no one ever acknowledged the first donation. Expressing gratitude goes a long way in fostering a strong relationship with your donors. Conveying your gratitude will allow your donors to know they are seen by you regardless of the amount. This should not only be reserved for those who give a larger amount, this should be extended to every donor. You never know what someone has that they are not disclosing. That person may be the person that consistently gives $20 a month; however, there estate may have your organization as a primary beneficiary, unbeknownst to you. So never dismiss extending a thank you to any donor.

Thanking your donors can be done in different ways as well. Here are some tips:

1. Send a monthly newsletter recognizing a different donor each month.
2. Host a Donor Appreciation Dinner

3. Phone your donors to express gratitude and appreciation (this should not be done by a volunteer; this should be executed by the executive director or a board member)
4. Send thank you letters between 24-48 hours after a donation has been made to show the organization's gratitude

The following quote struck a chord with me as it drives home the point of nurturing those helping you in your cause. "Feeling gratitude and not expressing it is like wrapping a present and NOT giving it." – William Author Ward

CHAPTER 9

If It Don't Make Dollars, It Don't Make Sense: Money Management

"You will either learn to manage money, or the lack of it will manage you!"

– Dave Ramsey

Managing funds within a nonprofit must be above reproach. This should be the case with ANY business. However, as nonprofits handle large amounts of donor funds, the organization's fiduciary responsibility is to ensure that they manage funds impeccably. There are nuances between a for-profit and a non-profit. One such difference is that a nonprofit's tax returns are public record while an LLC or Sole Proprietors are not. So, as you earn and generate donations/money for the organization, your funds management must be thorough and impeccably kept.

First and foremost, if you have a for-profit and a non-profit, make sure the funds NEVER co-mingle. If the for-profit company must lend money to the nonprofit for any reason, a designated individual should document it in a record and the meeting minutes. They should log details such as the date and repayment means. They should record it as an instrument that can leave a paper trail like a check. Everything should be documented in preparation for an internal or external audit.

Managing money should not be a guessing game. Clear instructions should be provided to the person responsible for fund management. In most cases, this is the treasurer's role. The organization should provide a clear job description during the recruitment process for transparency. At minimum, they should include the following:

1. A monthly financial report for board meeting presentation, which will include details on funds and expenses, including salaries, supplies, etc.
2. Bank statements with details on storage and accessibility.
3. Instructions regarding the ability to have "petty cash"
4. Instructions on check signatures (e.g., two or one signature on checks)

This avoids not knowing where and how your organization uses money. It also provides transparency within the organization, which gives the board of directors the confidence to ask for donations, knowing the funds are used as advertised. Having multiple bank accounts in the organization's name is also good practice. Why is this? It allows for a check and balance. It allows things to make sense. Here are the various bank accounts a nonprofit should have:

1. **An Operating Account (Main Account)**. This should be the main account for paying monthly bills and operating expenses.
2. **A Fundraising Account**. This account should be solely dedicated to holding funds generated from fundraisers, campaigns, etc. This is a great way to manage your accumulated funds for each fundraiser.
3. **A Payroll Account**. This is when you secure staff. This is not an account that needs to open right away. When you first begin, you may not have the budget for salaried positions. However, once you expand and grow, you can open one to ensure payroll is handled efficiently. If you opt to have a payroll company handle payroll, they can manage direct deposits, 1099's, W-2's and W-9's. They require a separate payroll account to handle that.
4. **Petty Cash (Optional)**. Some organizations have a petty cash account with a certain dollar amount so that in last-minute situations where items must be purchased at a nominal cost, a nonprofit does not need to conduct a board meeting to vote on purchasing small items here and there. If a receipt is provided for what was purchased for the organization's benefit, a petty cash account allows small necessary withdrawals without pause.

If you receive a solicitation for something that does not make sense, do **not** do it. Err on the side of caution. You will never go wrong. When handling money, you want to guarantee no funny business is happening.

Many aspiring founders ask me if they can be paid to run a Non-Profit organization. Simply put, the answer is YES. However, there are some conditions to earning a salary for a nonprofit you founded. For some, it takes an adjustment, but avoiding a conflict of interest is necessary and, more importantly, maintaining the organization's integrity is always at the forefront.

A founder usually begins as one of the board of directors. However, when one wants to earn a salary from the organization, they can no longer have a vote, which is one of the main objectives to being a board member. When you become an employee of the organization, you can no longer vote because that would require you to vote on your salary and cause a conflict of interest. Most founders take the position of the organization's executive director, which holds a lot of weight.

The board of directors and volunteers answer to the executive director. You are the face of the organization, the main advocate, the go-to. While you are required to attend board meetings and provide a perspective, you do not have a vote. Please do not think that your voice does not hold weight because it does. Your salary would come from the executive director's position.

How you determine your salary may depend on how much the organization generates each year. Clearly, your salary would differ from the Red Cross's executive director, who makes six figures. As a grassroots nonprofit, your salary would be comparable to another nonprofit with the same budget. The good news is as your organization grows, so can your salary. You would be required to do more, so your salary should reflect that. If you need help with how to calculate your salary estimate, you have several options that can help.

You can call the IRS and ask about comparable salaries within your budget. You can go to a staffing agency and ask the same question. Alternatively, you can go on Indeed.com and review job descriptions for grassroots nonprofits or Guidestar.com. Financial reports are public record, so you will be able to see an Executive Director's salary. These are great sources to refer to when making these determinations.

If ever audited, the IRS will see if the organization pays salaries and contributes to programs appropriately. The money that is raised through donations, fundraisers, and campaigns can be used for salary, operating, and administrative expenses. Some grants may help as well. If a grant is restricted to programs only, then the organization can only use the funds as designated. If you are awarded an unrestricted grant, you can use it for whatever the organization deems is necessary, including salary.

CHAPTER 10

The Burn Out: Work Smarter, Not Harder

"Burnout is not about giving too much of yourself, it's about trying to give what you do not possess!"

In the nonprofit world, it is far too easy to burn out. Visionaries often see exactly how they want things, but often cannot articulate that vision in a way that allows others to follow and implement it. The effect then is frustration and shutting down, and it becomes an "I'll just do it myself" thing, a recipe for disaster. No successful person has accomplished that success without the assistance from others. Isolation does not breed success and working on the "island onto myself" mentality doesn't contribute to legacy building or succession.

In speaking with leaders and remembering my early days of leadership, understanding the difference between management and leadership was a foreign concept. Therefore, I could not implement them appropriately to get the most and bring out the best in my team. Burnout happens when you first do not recognize your limitations. Leaders often have an "end-all-be-all" mindset, which is not sustainable.

Here is where bringing out the best in others comes into play for the betterment of your organization. If you know your vision requires a certain skill set and you do not possess that skillset, your job is to find the right person. You then articulate your vision and inform the person who possesses the talent, how they can contribute to the success of that vision and how that would impact the organization's recipients. That is inspiring someone and bringing out the best in them.

Managing the process is when you inspect what you expect while setting clear expectations of what you are looking for. Check in from time to time. Do not micromanage, but help as needed. Sometimes, collaborating thoughts can help someone bring your vision to life. Overseeing the process creates more time for you to focus on new efforts and nurture existing ones. When you check in from time to time, it also alleviates frustration when something is done incorrectly or inefficiently. A redirection or clarification may be needed to ensure the desired result occurs.

No one wants to do things incorrectly when they understand the effect their actions can have on so many lives. Constructive feedback is welcomed, especially when the intention to help is genuinely expressed. That is managing, which is different from leading and inspiring. The late Mother Theresa said it so eloquently when she said, "You can do what I cannot do! I can do what you cannot do! Together we can do great things."

What you need to learn how to do, your resources and team can streamline how to do it. That is the foundation of working smarter, not harder. We can take the scenic route to get to the end goal, or we can take the shorter more efficient way to get to the same end goal without feeling exhausted upon arrival.

This also creates a perfect merging of the old and the new and what will one day be the ones leading and managing the nonprofit you founded. This is called succession planning. I love how Anne M Mucahy described succession. She said, "one of the things we often miss in the succession planning is that it should be gradual and thoughtful, with lots of sharing of information and knowledge and perspective, so that it's almost a non-event when it happens!"

When you can inspire and direct those to assist in helping your organization move forward, it takes a wealth of sharing and mentoring. Many organizations have been stopped dead in its tracks because of an unforeseen removal of a key person within the organization and having no one who could pick up the baton to keep it going…what a shame! When one knows, they can teach…each one, teach one right?

Are you delegating and teaching appropriately to avoid burnout? A sign you are leading without burnout is when you can leave for a period, and the organization is still running smoothly. A sign you are on the verge of a burnout is when you feel you cannot remove yourself because everything will fall apart not realizing one of those things is YOU! You must realize that you have a team of competent members working for you and alongside you. Not having a competent team or not trusting that they will fulfill their duties will contribute to your path to burning out.

Below is a list of signs of burnout. If you are experiencing these symptoms, sit with your executive team to strategize getting talent to share the responsibilities.

Signs of Burnout

1. You have become cynical or critical. This would be the opposite of the corporate culture you desire. Charitable work is a good feel, so if coming to work creates this critical and cynical mood, this may be a sign that you are working harder, not smarter.
2. Do you drag yourself into board meetings, networking events? Do you avoid them?
3. Have you become irritable or short with members of your board or volunteers?
4. Have you become more physically tired due to mental exhaustion?
5. Do you have brain fog? A lack of concentration?
6. Do you feel like you are on a hamster wheel going nowhere? Do you feel busy, but not productive?
7. Do you suffer from physical ailments that you did not before that are often associated with stress, like headaches, stomach pains, or insomnia?

The best way to avoid this is by being honest with yourself. Drop the ego and the justification that says "I'll just do it myself if I want it done right." Instead, what you should be saying is how can I articulate my vision and expectations more efficiently to attain the results needed and allow me some time so that I can have balance? This may not be easy to swallow as you read along, but attitude amongst your team reflects LEADERSHIP or the lack thereof. That is the beauty of potential burnout. You can turn it around, but it starts with you first.

Be honest with yourself in terms of identifying what areas you can improve upon and immediately begin implementing ways in which to evolve. If there is anything constant, it is change. Change is good. It promotes growth and development, which is exciting and always evolving. This is a corporate culture most want to be a part of.

This change may require seeking a business coach to help you along the way. Remember, work smarter, not harder. If seeking a coach is outside your budget, listen to business podcasts on subjects you need to improve on, find resources to read or speak to someone who has done it before. One of the things I used to do in my corporate days that I have since utilized in my nonprofit work is I will reach out to someone excelling in an area I know I need to improve, and I ask them if they can share their advice with me.

Now, you may think that a person in such a position would not provide you support. However, from personal experience, that could not be further from the truth. Why? You have expressed to that person that you view them as the blueprint, someone you look up to as a guiding light in your field. Leaders love to share best practices. If this does not work for you, start networking, get in the room with successful people. Observe, take notes, and implement the BEST practices you see for success.

You cannot bring your vision forth if you become too worn out to lead the mission. When you share your story, you share the alternative to the solution you are bring forth. So many nonprofit founders will face negative effects by failing to make necessary adjustments for you to keep going. Do not let that happen! You can turn it around. Tell your brain that so that it will prove you right!

In conclusion, if reading this makes you feel like you have a lot of work to do, I have fulfilled my intention with this book. Charitable work is often misconstrued when people leave off the word "work." By having that intention of working hard and buying this book, you have taken two excellent steps in the right direction.

Anything you pray for; you must work for. God cannot bless what does not exist, so give him something to bless while you pray with good intentions about your work to positively impact the lives you wish to change in a desirable direction. I wrote this book to change the picture we have in our minds that has held us back from doing some amazing work. I took my paint brush and started a new portrait with new colors. Will you and your organization pick up your brushes and complete a new portrait with new information and guidelines?

Our communities need it the most, so why not put in the most to change that? Our mantra in my boutique consulting firm is "First we help you learn…then drop the "L."

Notes

Notes

Notes

Notes

Notes

Utopian Enterprise Offers…

Non-Profit Masterclass

This is a 12-week course that teaches each participant how to start a Non-Profit correctly as well as after creating the Non-Profit; how to run it effectively and efficiently for maximum results. Classroom topics include, but are not limited to Board Development, Volunteer Management, Obtaining Corporate Funding and Storytelling. The Masterclass concludes with a Business Plan Presentation amongst successful entrepreneurs. Each student receives a Certificate of Completion.

This course is taught 4 times a year, January, April, June, September. Please visit our website to sign up for the Masterclass at www.utopianenterprisebiz.com

Executive Coaching

This service provides one on one coaching with the Founder, Executive Director or Board of Directors. One on one coaching includes Leadership and Delegation training along with strategic planning for next level results. We can also provide customized training in areas of improvement. To set up a consultation, please visit our website to sign up at www.utopianenterprisebiz.com

Teambuilding/Development

Utopian Enterprise provides team building workshops that will create an environment of trust and productivity amongst team members. These workshops are customized around the personalities of each member which allows a safe space of growth and understanding; utilizing one another's strengths while not focusing on the weaknesses. This service is offered both virtually and face to face. To set up a teambuilding day for your team, visit our website at www.utopianenterprisebiz.com

Grant Writing

This service is only available to Non-Profit organizations that possess their 501c3 Tax Exempt status. This service provides grant writing for:

1. Community Grants
2. Foundations
3. City Proposals
4. Federal/Government Grants
5. General Restricted/Non-Restricted Grants.

This service is offered on a continual basis for a guaranteed number of grants submitted per month of which a contract will be created, or one can retain this service for one grant that your organization is seeking additional aid from. To obtain this service, please visit our website at www.utopianenterprisebiz.com

Fundraising Specialist

This service will help nonprofit organizations develop an ongoing campaign strategy for securing funds. This service will guide clients through the aspects of planning and running effective fundraising campaigns that include nurturing relationships to cultivate long term funding.

Become a Utopian Member

This membership will provide a 15% discount on our monthly webinars and Utopian events, weekly emails of upcoming networking events and grant opportunities which will include the link to the grant application. A monthly newsletter is also included along with 30-minute consultations with Non-Profit Strategist, Asiya Nasir.

Made in the USA
Middletown, DE
04 July 2024

56824502R00058